In Search of a Way Beyond the Clouds

by

Mina Rahravan

Bloomington, IN Milton Keynes, UK

authorHOUSE®

AuthorHouse™
1663 Liberty Drive, Suite 200
Bloomington, IN 47403
www.authorhouse.com
Phone: 1-800-839-8640

AuthorHouse™ UK Ltd.
500 Avebury Boulevard
Central Milton Keynes, MK9 2BE
www.authorhouse.co.uk
Phone: 08001974150

First published by AuthorHouse 9/13/2006

ISBN: 1-4259-6281-5 (sc)

Printed in the United States of America
Bloomington, Indiana

This book is printed on acid-free paper.

Cover design: Maryam Rahravan

The flame of this prose is rising from the bottom of my heart and I hope it touches you with a gentle warmth to the untouched depth of your beautiful heart!

To everything
there is a season
and to my love for you.

To you,

more than before

more than ever!

For years
It was your world
                and I lovingly lived in it.
It was your path
                and I happily walked through it.
For years
You were my only sun
And I was one of the countless moons
Gratefully living around you
                        and madly orbiting
For years
You were the sky
And I was the only enamored bird
                        Cheerfully flying within you
overcoming your winds.
I thought of you, when rain came
I dreamed about you, when night fell
And when day arrived, I woke up for you.

For you, for years
The glass door of my heart
Was locked and never opened
            unless knocked by you.
There was no love prose,
                no love poem
                        unless for you.
I cried and cried your deepest sorrows,
I chanted your songs
and I smiled at your joys.

For years, you strummed and stroked
The delicate strings
of my fragile soul.
You chose to disappear for so many years

And I proudly became
                your unheard voice.
You were my world
                for years and years.

But there comes a day
        when you hear the roaring waves of the sea
                as you walk between the lines of this prose.

There comes a day
        when you hear the whisper of that cool spring gale
                that woke me up
                        and made me alive again,
                                with life's precious alchemies on a tray.

A time may come
when I fill the emptiness of your room
                with the same pure smell of those rain drops
                        that kept falling and falling
                        on the thirsty soil of
                                that far deserted land,
                                        on that brisk cold autumn day.

When that day arrives, I will capture you in my arms
                and I will carry you in the air
                        to the unknown world of my wildest dreams.

I shine on you, when the sun shines
I fall on you, when rain falls.
I become one with the rays and I shower my glorious glare
On all of those mystic nights
When the moon lights generously
on all of your ways.
I twinkle in every star
that shines before you
in the vast field of dark velvet sky.

I sparkle, I float in the clouds, I weave into the fogs.
I become aroma, I rise from the rose,
I selflessly dissolve myself in the air
and every single time that you breath in the air
You hear me knocking.
I knock on your stone-hearted door.

One day I embody the sea,
One day when you walk on my coast,
with one overwhelming flow,
I will steal you from yourself
And take you to my world.
I sail you in my soul ,
and there, in the middle of my waves,
I surround you,
crawl on you,
touch you,
smell you,
cherish you,
 kiss you
 and like a careless breeze I pass you and I leave you behind.

What if the memory of that kiss
        haunts you day and night
                and steals you forever from your heart?

What if your eyes become everlastingly restless and tearful like
mine?

What if this time around
        I choose the writing
                and you become the knight?

What if this time,
 I write you the role and create your path and you follow my lead
and march any forbidden roads that I command?

What if at last,
        before the story ends,
                in those seasons and chapters,
                        somewhere in nowhere,
                                when your clamor arises,
                                        when you rave and roar
                                                and you mount on your horse
                                                        when you strive to soar,
I storm through the pages
        by the dust of the wind
                blown by the hooves of your own fast thunder
steed?
What if I terminate this ode,
        close your fables and epic tales and forever leave you lost
and unread behind?

This is where it starts…
                So, more than ever welcome to my world!

And what a distance between the green of this land and the calm green of your eyes.

What a gap between the blue of this sky
                    And the amorous blue of your eyes,

It took me a single glance
            of your gazelle eyes
                    to fall into your world
but a lifetime
            it will take
                    to fly back to my nest
                            and to calm
                                    my enamored soul.

What is on your mind
  that I am so restless tonight?

You are breezing through my mind …Years have passed now, and still no matter what season of the year and what time of the day and what stage of my life, I still think about you.

If not now then when would be the greatest time to share with you what I felt without you in the two seasons of my life when I blossomed and when I fell.

It is one cold autumn day. I am lying freely on the white smooth sands beside the sea. I am bare, as bare as the bareness of my being. I am unconscious, I am numb, I feel as if I never existed.

The smooth passage of the breeze is touching my skin and my heartbeats are in tremendous harmony with the tides of the sea. My soul is finetuned with the whole universe. Again, the revolutionary autumn has arrived when the leaves fall.
But I blossom!

I am contemplating the sea and seagulls; sea shells are floating on the foamy waves of the surface of the sea awaiting that single rain drop that carries that unborn pearl inside. The wind is constantly blowing underneath the wide wings of the seabirds and I am observing the sky and the clouds.

The sky is full of dark grey clouds marching slowly towards each other, getting close and closer, but not yet close enough to become rain and fall.

I wish I had this rest in the fast spin of my life. To close my eyes only for a while and to experiment this magnificent feeling of being so entirely present in the wide width of these magical moments. I wish I had had the privilege earlier to rest my head against the gentle shoulders of Mother Earth, to calm my soul with the melody of her heart.

Thunder...

Lightning....

The symphony of the rain starts...

My heart bleeds.
My body trembles.
I am soaked and cold by this rain.
I can hear myself breath.
I put my hands on my temples.
I feel the pulse.
Am I alive?
A cascade of tears
Start falling from my eyes.
I am tired
but still gazing at the clouds,
in search of a way
to reach you my love,
beyond these clouds…

...Once upon a time, the strong hands of the wind, carried by chance, the body of a seed to the driest soil of an uncharted land and left it alone among millions upon millions of grains of sand...

...and I couldn't sleep. I could hear the fast heartbeats of the nightingale wandering fearfully from one side to the other in the small alleys of our neighborhood. Where were you on that cold dark autumn night?

How many times were we led to the doorway of our dreams by the hands of a fairy mermaid or a prince coming from one of those fake heaven lands?

How many years they got us to believe in those heavenly sculpted angels, unreal heroes and virtual beings?

How many times did we stay up in bed gazing at the sky, hoping those flying angels would come down to our land, take us in their hands and fly us to the heights of their heavens? Did they not know that in the convulsion of restless nights, we needed an open window, fresh air, we needed a breeze to open up the door of our little hearts to let our stories float in the ether. We did not need the obligation of hearing the repeated myths.

And here is another moonless night, another restless child far away from the sweet, colorful world of dreams.

And why is that the most delicate and fragile flowers grow without
     The admiring eyes of a gardener
                  or the warm touch of watering hands?

Why is that they grow freely
              on driest slopes
                  roadsides
                        or the wasted lands?
Why is it that their life is gone
              with the careless touch
                  of a plucking hand!

Dream has become that wild deer running away from her eyes.

She was let too early out of the children's world. Falling asleep is just a far away dream.

There was no moon to lighten the darkness of her night, she was unrecognizable even to herself. These are the last pages of the tale and she has not yet fallen asleep.

Angels were fake, they didn't exist. They never left the height of their throne to come down to our land and to decorate our world with their presence and to beautify the fantasies of our earthy land.

We never felt their company on those lonely nights. They never told us the secrets of the world and never eased the consistent agitation of our disillusioned minds.

Weren't those stories supposed to be bridges for us to cross so we would reach the land of dreams? Had they not known that we were anxious to fly? Maybe even angels have fallen asleep.

God, how many sheep to count before the children across the world finally fall asleep every night?

After years of being repeated and read, those stories had no more pulse, they weren't alive.

How many times did we fight for those most gleaming stars of those starry nights, wanting to hide or possess their bigness in the small palm of our little hands? No one ever said that those sparkles are only the lights of the stars that have disappeared thousands of light years ago.

How many times did I sleep with that sweet illusion that I got my share from the seven skies and I slept after I filled my hands full of stars? How many times did I wake up and my heart was in sorrow when I opened my empty hands on the morrow?

It was a lie.

They ornamented our nights with unreal fables.

There never came an angel to fly her far from her bed. Maybe angels were just flying asleep.

The heavy silence of the night is broken by the voice of the storyteller but it is not easy to believe...

And those restless children of today
        are the heroes of the true myths of tomorrow.
Those that never ceased questioning
        and observed through the window of their curious eyes
                are the ones who will return with answers to our
big questions of tomorrow...

It's midnight.

The sea wrinkles its wild beautiful face to the rough touch of this wind. Curtains of dark clouds slowly disperse the beauty of the moon and the sky. I can hear the leaves of the shore-trees murmuring rumors brought by this telltale wind about the sea and the story of her endless passion and helpless love for reaching the sky.

I sit on the sand, I am watching the sea. I look into your feverous eyes. Lest I sleep and disloyal wind swipes you away from my dreams!

I stare at the clouds. The moon helplessly gave up in her duel with the clouds. Tears keep falling from my eyes. If I were a painter, with the magic of my painting brush, my skies would never have clouds. I draw two lines on the white sands by the sea and make a bird...

I wish I were a painter.

I traveled years and years
for the bluest eyes of the sky.
The sky was my world,
my dream land,
my paradise
And you brought that far distant blue
Down on the whiteness of your canvas
            with a gentle
                        touch of your brush.

I wish I were a painter.

I was tired of this soil,
I was longing to grow powerful wings to fly with
            You draw thousands of wild seagulls above your sea.
You colored your brush in the rainbow
And you painted royal falcons
                        Hovering in the blue kingdom of your sky.

I walked
The un-walked roads
            of those furthest lands
In search of green.
And you glanced at the palest yellow
                        With those legendary blue of your eyes,
                                    and you made green.
        Ah! How good it is to be a painter.
                    What an amazing world, your world should be.
What a tremendous victorious pride to draw.
                        How I wish I were a painter!

As if everything
is an abstract work of art
the wild imaginations
of a hidden brush

Fire red, blue, yellow, grey, violet, black and white-
The sunset keeps coloring the clouds.
It's constantly changing,
Not even one single repeated design
as if the hand of the artist is drawing images
                    out of an endless collection of originality.

The story teller kept telling stories
        but the child was not hearing anything.
        She had her own stories
          a loud voice
            a roar in her silent world…

To be heard,
   To be the rage of a generation
   Not the quiet murmur of a lonely
      child!

There was nothing but darkness in her world, there was no crack to let in any rays of light to open up a window to the world. All she could feel was the touch of the breeze that could roll the delicate body of our baby seed on the surface of the soil. What a feeling !Traveling weightlessly in the cradle of those tremendously kind hands of a breeze without destination on this land and without a desire to rest.

The breeze flew her through the clouds, traveled her soul in the same direction as the sun. She told her from falling rivers and their never ending travel towards the sea. From migrating swallows that are the first messengers of spring, from the mystery of dawns, when the world wakes up to the light of the day and the miraculous beauty of every dusk when our sun leaves us alone in darkness to magically enlighten the horizon of another land.

She talked about darkness and light, from weeping candles and their burning flames and the story of her famous quest for lighting the dark burdens with her little shimmering light. She spoke of shooting stars, of why they travel and those unfamiliar territories where they fall.

Of all the stories she heard and all the places that she traveled she found one story similar to hers.

One day she will encounter the admirable candle light and she will crack herself open to her light. One day she will settle in the beauty of a meadow to sprout. One day she will proudly flower.

She made her mind up to stay strong through the slow passage of the days and nights and to keep the greatness of her soul nourished by the thoughts of this morning breeze. One day she will get out of the prison of her shell and celebrate herself while beginning her life.

I am far from you
But I am there beside you.
I am numb
  but still feel your pain.
I am frightened by this wild storm
    And struggle hard
     To move against the strong force of this stubborn wind
        to reach you and cross the waves of the sea
    and a soft breeze smoothly
       tickles the corner of your sleeping eye.

I lie on the sands,
    I whisper your name and I close my eyes.
     You hear your name,
       shiver in your bed
        and you open your eyes…

We are both
   sailors on the same sea tonight.
     Maybe somewhere
       Sometime
      During this surfing duet
       in the middle
         or at the end of the sea,
    Maybe on the razor-sharp edge of the horizon
     Where the earth cuddles in the arms of the sky
       I embrace you and kiss your eyes.

And one day the breeze came in stronger than all those virtual heroes and took me in her arms to another sky, to another land where those shooting stars used to fall and where the stars are reborn. She took me to the land where the sun, moon and the stars are sleeping amorously in the velvet bed of the sky. She breezed me through the stars and I brought thousands of stars home. My hands are small but they are the cradle of millions of stars. I have traveled with the breeze. We have shared the same destinations.

She has told me stories. I know the secret of the blue of the sky, I know the why of the restlessness of this agitated wind, I know towards which sky the sun travels when it hides and descends. I know why the rivers rebel and the streams are so calm. I know why the rivers constantly desire to free themselves from the tight and narrowed boundaries of their banks. I know why they long to reach the sea.

The breeze has talked to me about a small migrating bird that has lost her heart to the purest green of spring, a black bird with a white patch on her chest that travels above the lands as a messenger of the spring. I know stories from swallows, I know the secret of their mission.

How can I close my eyes when the whole universe is awake and changing at a glance of my eyes? What if I sleep! What a pity to close my eyes to this moon light. How can I close my eyes to this morning breeze that crosses my sky while I am asleep? The moon is our guest only for a few hours and the sun is traveling towards the horizon, setting out for another sky.

The night wasn't as empty as she thought, the city is asleep but the night, with all it's miraculous wonders is awake: Nightingales are singing! The sea is alert and awake, breathing. The wind whistles. Sea oats are dancing to the passage of the wind. Night is perfumed by the roses and golden chains. Clouds are dancing on the stage of the sky. You can hear the steps of the nightwalkers! Shining fireflies glow, hop and fall. Streams are dancing through the stones, trees are breathing, leaves are shaking and singing to the wind.

Your town is asleep but a galaxy of shining stars is staying awake above these clouds.

Colorful leaves are falling gently on the bed of the earth. Trees, drunk by the touch of the breeze, are weeping their yellow leaves. It's the play of color and light on the stage of the sky. Snow white clouds crawl gently, releasing their tears. Rain starts falling from the blue eyes of the sky. Sea oats bow to the wake of the storm and passage of the whirling wind. The sky is still the paradise for the able flyers and wild seagulls. A flock silently passes against the direction of the dominant wind over the coast! Golden chains shake and tremble. Little birds are rapidly flapping their wings to overcome the winds and hawks are at the height of the sky weightlessly riding on the wind and floating up and down in the air. The sea is breathing loud, embracing the sands with tremendously huge tides. The secrecy of nature's art of love is bare in hands of the violent wind caressing the weeping willows...

Either the calmness of a "Sweet Stillness" or a "Destructive Tornado" is the crop.

Lest the sleep takes the alertness away from your eyes! Open up your wings, prepare to fly, as beyond the chaos of these clouds there is nothing but pure awakeness and clarity of sky. A galaxy full of stars is shining somewhere above these clouds.

Don't close your eyes!

Tell me the life story of the Shooting stars.
When did they start falling?
Tell me of that unknown land, where they fall.

Tell me of those long distance migrating swallows.
Of those sole messengers of the spring!
When did their long journey start?
How long have they been carrying the message of spring?
Tell me if they ever weave together a nest?
Do they ever rest on the twigs of the trees?
Have you ever heard them?
Do they ever sing?

And I wasn't alone
  but I was so lonely without you,
    Like the moon in the sea of the
      stars...

How can I sleep tonight? Someone must guard you tonight.

I must write you tonight, for one last time I must dream you into being.

Come beside me before the sleep takes me away.

From the sky
   down to the earth
      It took us the cry of a birth.
From the earth to the height of the
   sky
      It took us the time of a life.

And what a journey!

Crossing those unknown lands, with you, in search of green!

From the northest north to the bottom south.

What a journey!
            With you, chasing the eternal trail of the sun, ascending
from the East and never descending.

The city was small,
        Too small for you
                to spread your giant wings,
        too small for you to free your soul and to freely fly,
too small to squeeze your bigness inside its tight borders…

No gardener
            But we grew.
No teacher
            But we were able flyers
We fell and fell
            But still seek our way
                to the stars…

What a joy to ride on the wind and to sail in the wide open sky
above the clouds!

We ascent
        In the light of the sun rise.
                    We went up and up
                        Towards the edge of horizon.
                        We flew into the sunrise
                            until we disappeared
                            like a dot.
                        We became invisible
                        in the blank page of the sky.

And the city that took me a life to travel from one side to another
was small.
     Smaller
         than a tear drop
             from above.

And our land, our alleys, streams and rivers, all of our trees and flowers, ourselves and heights of the seven skies were under our wings.

How glorious, to pass with you from those never ending roads in the sky!
How charming it was to travel with you through mountains, from forests to dry deserted lands.

How great to satisfy this old craze to discover with you the wonders of the sky.

How beautiful it was to search with you my forgotten self. How wonderful to pass this planet side by side with you.

I felt weightless every time I carried the lightness of your being in my arms. I flew in the skies each time I kissed the deep beauty of your eyes.

We traveled and watched the cattle

grazing the green grass,

their faces towards the earth,

their back towards the blue of the

sky.

And one day it will be green
all those red lights that we fearlessly
crossed.

Our voyage started from the dawn of time. It's been years since we have been engraving the story of our lives on the wide old tables of the discovery walk trails that pass and curve through our lands. Everyone wrote the story in her own way, that once upon a time …

Some passed and wondered at the wall, some wrote and passed by the wall and some never even noticed the existence of that wall.

The wheel of time turned and turned and it came our turn to pass those unknown roads.

And what was life to our eyes? It was ongoing poem that was enormously pleasing to our hearts.

We were hypnotized by those patterns, we marveled at the images, and those lyrics were as harmonious as a well written poem. We became the joyful inheritors of an old poem whose rhyme was lost so we lived according to what the worldly ancients wrote.

You whispered in my ears that the travelers of today are tomorrow's dream makers.

When we walked, everything walked; when we stopped, everything stopped. We had the desire to listen and with us, everything was capable of talking.

By touching those handmade carpets and rugs, we touched the hands that wove those rugs.

How could we walk on the lines of those artist hands?

We rested on them, we rested our face against the face of the miniature images…

We heard the quiet humming of the weaver who lived through those warps and woofs.

We heard her when on those grey cloudy days she cried.

We heard her when she laughed.

We felt it when she smiled

We fell asleep
        In the warmth of her bereaved hands.
                When we woke up,
We were lost
In the depth of the lines
                of the spinner's hands.

We traveled and traveled
        and the cattle
                were still grazing.

You're falling on me in every single
water drop.

Come to me!

Before it's too late!

Before this wind carries the
alertness from my eyes!

Flowering?

     In that wilderness of a land!

    It was just a far,

            far away dream.

 It became her quest.

Even if it takes her life to tear her thick skin open,

        she would sprout and blossom.

           She would unfold her life to the light.

Her dreams were growing bigger than the small world of a seed, but fearless, she was to believe in her impossible dream.

That was all she desired from this entire world: to crack open, breath in fresh air, flower one day and become green.

She grew tall, taller than a seed. She never covered her face from the sun. She watered her soul with her tears. She was just a different seed. She would close her eyes when the dry eyes of the desert were cracking open and when the desert was asleep she was chatting with the breeze. She didn't follow the command of the hands of any clock. She didn't belong to this desert, she was brought over here. One day, sooner or later, she will depart from this land...

I chose you before I was born.

I heard your questions before you voiced them, I danced with you, step by step, hand in hand, side by side, when in the turning point of your life, you danced as you walked those roads. I was there beside you, but I was too small to be seen.

I wish I had been born earlier!

You echo in the wind,
       in the rain,
          in my soul.

How can I possibly unwind all the emotions and thoughts and feelings that have woven the fabric of my soul into being. Every smell, every sound, every touch and every single sign from inside and outside let me sink into your thoughts.

                 Alas we couldn't last together!

I wonder why is it that the most heart pleasing singing birds
sing only on the highest twigs
of the tallest trees?

Why do they amorously sing
from the birth of the light at dawn
until its farewell at dusk?

What do they see?
What do they sing for?

How come they sing
as lovingly as the first time they saw
the magic of the sunrise or the sunset?

For birds,
there is always a beloved flower to sing for,
there is always a love to live for.
There is always a tremendous beauty to observe from up there
And to constantly
Celebrate, sing and admire.
Birds live their life
as if it was the last day of their lives.

Remember those small alleys full of Red Roses, Violas and Bleeding hearts?

Remember those orioles and larks? They used to sit and sing on the highest twigs of the tallest trees of the neighborhood.

We tuned our guitars to their sounds and under the moonlight we played along with their songs. Birds nestled on our trees. Remember their babies bird that were madly flapping their wings before they started their first fly? We were the guardians of those passionate symbols of flying. Lest they fall and never follow their dream! We called every single singing bird by name, to us they were singing passionately knowing that there are two pairs of curious eyes watching them, admiring them. How many springs were we the uninvited guests of their ongoing feast of life with all its loving beings?

We were the only passer-bys of that heaven full of larks.

We sent them our love through our eyes without frightening them,

but there were eyes lying
        in ambush
                for the beauty of their songs.

We saw patterns on the wall, we carved our way into the past and in search of that melodic rhyme.

We happily reiterated all of the ancient words. We kept singing the old songs until we captured the rhythm. We made bridges from the present to the past.

Remember those one-day flies with a simple purpose to their one day life, from dawn till the dusk, flying around the pale light of any lit lanterns. Flying around it until the end of their life.

How many lanterns did you lighten on your way?

When did we start the journey towards growing green?

We have been walking on this planet for years now. We have carved our fantasies on the old plain walls of our cities, we didn't pass watching, we drew a line, we passed singing our songs. We made bridges from the past to now, for us, to reach the sky.

And Dandelions were brave travelers, like us, crossing the tall walls and entering other lands to rest in someone's hand. We could feel in the palm of our hands, the weight of the wishes and desires that they were carrying in the lightness of their fairy being.

There was always someone wishing for something from a far away land and to fly them in the air and set them off to dream lands. Dandelions had no border to cross.

Every time we came across those light travelers we paused, we welcomed them and we carried them with so much care and love in our hands and set them off with our love wishing to bring back good news to those who lived in the depth of uncharted lands.

We were all connected to each other through these fairy flying messengers, no matter where we were, we were communicating with each other through these beautiful tireless flowery travelers.

I have sent

    fields of dandelions to the sky.

      They all carry the same wish!

        Come to me!

One day she slept but there was something at her feet, as if the earth came up and crawled onto her feet. She could not roll by the blow of the breeze, she was not round, not free to roll her soul.

God, help me! I can feel the massive weight of my being.

There was nothing wrong at all, the storyteller said. She was rooting in the earth, that is how the seeds grow.

The breeze that let her taste the lightness of the being, planted her feet firmly on the dry harsh body of the ground.

Like the lonely star that shines in the last minutes of darkness in the sky, the seed started to blossom in her solitude and grew.

Walking to the light of the candle became a far
    far
     far
      far away dream!

I feel the autumn by the bareness of the garden, black crows are the only fruits grown on the naked body of the trees.

The sky is clouded by huge layers of fog,
      There is no sign of the swallows;
            orioles and larks are hunted by hawks.

Eaglets are not eager to practice the flight, they are happy with worms as their prey. Instead of pure streams, they drink from the swamps. Fountains are unknown to their eyes!

The soil has forgotten how to grow again, the arrival of the spring has become a far away dream.

Passerbys shelter themselves from the rain, they cover themselves from the sun, they close their windows to the sound of the loving birds.

The city is surrounded by highrises and no one has windows, no one ever minds the lack of view.

Autumn cries.

I am crying.

Waves washed my bird away from the sands.

Everything is drawn into the bottom of the sea. I hand you my tears to wipe off everything and to draw me your art on the whiteness of my heart.

I am waiting for night to give birth to the light of day. I won't sleep tonight.

Believing you is impossible!

Tears ambush your dark eyelashes.
Here are tears falling from my eyes.

The breeze waves your dark beautiful hair.
　　　　I smell the musk aroma of your scent in the air.

I feel cold.
　　　　　　I miss you
　　　　　　　　　　and the warmth
　　　　　　　　　　　　of your delicate body
　　　　　　　　　　　　　　in my arms...

And there came a day when three beautiful butterflies fell in love with the lonely flower of our story and her spirit of life, with her passion to grow and to become a plant. They praised her courage, they fed her with their love, they told her not to give up, to survive and to turn into a unique flower and to sit like a diamond in the center of the vast vase of this deserted soil.

The morning breeze that moved her and caressed her for years, put her finally in the soil, she could feel the weight of something above her.

How hard she tried not to fall asleep, how hard she tried to escape from this fall. There was always a sweet sorrow charming the beauty of her eyes.

The curtain of the night was jeweled by the endless number of stars but she was looking for that one reachable star.
Where is the candle?
        Where is her light?

Light up a candle!
 Become a mirror!
  Let yourself see the magnificence of your growth!
Don't give up!
Believe in your blossoms among the yellow dry leaves of the trees
who follow the rule and fall in autumn and blossom in spring.

Ah, lest you don't believe in yourself!

We branched apart
    and sulked in the air
        but our roots embraced
            in the depth of the same soil.
                Like trees!

We joyfully lived our life. Like two beloved butterflies, we fell in love with the beauty of every single flower that had grown out of the soil on this earth. But on the glorious petals of each flower we sat on there was always a hand waiting to grab our wings and take us away.

We were floating like a colorful rainbow on the blue font of the sky.

We became the gardener of a garden whose blossoms in the middle of autumn were only a myth among the ordinary flowers that blossomed in spring and died in fall.

We watered that flower of our orchard with our tears lest she withered and disappeared. We read stories to her of someone who tirelessly did not believe in the drought of any land and planted seeds of fire red roses on the bed of the desert, hoping that one day it would turn into a meadow or an ever green land.

Golden weeds danced beautifully to the passage of the desert breeze and we bent our soul to the wind to become a harp and play her life's sweetest melodies of impossible dreams.

Those eyes
that see and admire beauty
   are not any less than the beauty
   itself.

Days passed and passed in the life of that breathtakingly charming flower who was born lonely in the bed of a deserted land.

After the sunset the stunning butterflies sat on the delicate leaves of their flower listening to the whispers of their beloved one who was longing to see one thing in her entire life.

The only thing that was fascinating to her was nothing but the tremendous beauty of a candle that burns and still enlightens her surrounding world. She was so sad. Her life was too short and the desire of seeing the candle was so unreachable. She wished she were not a flower then she could walk. What it would be like to walk the whole planet in order to reach the light. But alas, she was just a flower meant to have roots in the depth of the soil. She is stuck in her own roots...

I am sinking in this sea tonight. I let go of myself. I may land dead or alive on that unknown island. We have both lost our way through this moonless night, we both gave up our faith to these roaring waves of the sea. We both lie in the arms of the sea, you, on one side, and I somewhere in the middle of the sea. You are as far from me as the sky is from the earth. Let these waves sail me to the fine border between the sea and the sky, let them carry me away to the edge of the horizon where the earth kisses the blue eyes of the sky. There I will shower you with the rain of my kisses.

The soil never woke up to the sound of the steps of spring breeze. Was there ever someone alive to join the season and celebrate the arrival of the spring?

No one will plant roses
      in the garden of your hands
            when you wake up every morning.

Roses are far away.
            I have no strength sleep is capturing my eyes.

I have no power to rush it
                     or to stop this flow.

The heavenly butterflies who heard the sobbing of the flower all day long would do anything, any thing in this world to make their star flower happy and to win her heart. So under the starry sky of that fine moonless night, the first butterfly opened up her gorgeous wings, looked up to the stars. To capture her love she flies off of her smooth gorgeous leaves in search of the light of a burning candle. For the sake of your beloved flower, there is no distance you would not travel. What a tremendous pleasure to see the candle and to be the first to tell of what is seen of light. He flies and flies and as soon his eyes are caught by an earthy light he turns back towards the flower to tell her all about the light and his discoveries.

Proud of his discovery, he lands slowly on the leaves of the flower. The flower who was eager to hear the story lets him lean in her arms and he starts telling his story.

It wasn't enough. The flower wasn't satisfied, her face shadowed with sorrow, she thought there must be more. He hadn't seen enough to describe the light of a candle. The flower was deeply saddened. She wished there was a force of some far world from ours, the force of a hand to pluck her from the stem and to take her to see the candle with her own eyes before she dies.

What are you made of?
Fire?
    Water?
        Air?
            Soil?
Which fire?

The one that warms the tired hands of a wood cutter on a summit
of the mountains?
Or from the fire of volcanoes that enflame the lands?

Which water?
    The one that springs from the purest fountains?
Or the water that runs like a flood out of the bed of rivers?

Which air?
The breeze that comes from heaven?
Or the one that turns and destroys the world?

Where did your soil come from?
            How did I fall into your hands?

You were the master of sculpture,
            the art of sculpting was truly in your hands
And I was the clay.

For years I climbed your hands
        I smelled your hands
                and I got drunk and fell.
                    I rested in the lines of your hands.
    I was that lifeless dry soil
    That was nourished by the shower of your tears.

You sculpted me in the finest details,
    You shaped me,
    contemplated me,
    Every time you took your eyes away from me,
            I fell,
                and disappeared.
I calmly kissed your hands
I climbed your hands, I flew
You revived me in your hands
You sang me sonorous songs and you cried
You mixed me with your tears
You shaped me with your thoughts.
You touched me gently, making me shine.
I shine like a glass I sparkle in your hands.
And you smiled at me with a glance
Through your dark beautiful eyes.

You empower my soil with your powerful soul.
You fill me, and lift me.
You raise and round me.
You take away my sharpest grains.
I wound your hands
And you humbly forget.
You rubbed your hands all around your face.
That is my chance -
To be that one happy little dust,
To sit on the corner of your stunning face.

I am drunk with your joyous warmth.
Keep, my love, keep taking me from myself.
You smoothen my being,
You breath your love into me
I fall and revive
With the touch of your hands
I wish I could crawl into your arms
Alas I am nothing but thousands of grains of sands
You are so proud that
I am all yours, right here in your hands
Shape me, mold me,
Destroy and re-make me
Create a bowl or make a pot
Come what may out of me
I am in your heart
Even if you leave me sitting unshaped
I become that dust
Falling at your feet
Every time the breeze blows

I still love your hands
I become cascade of kisses
And I keep falling on your hands
Like a wall-flower I grew to match the height of your love
I know no other way
Nothing other than your love

Unaware of our tale
Ignorant of the secrecy of our love
They took the clay from your hands
Many times they tried to shape things
Anything at all, out of the clay
Nothing was missing
Soil and water
Air and fire
But still
They failed

The clay exist only to her eyes
When she left the clay
The essence of its soil was taken away
No one ever succeeded
No one ever sculpted
And the smooth, soft clay
Became stone

Nothing came out
Life sulked
For ever and more than ever
They puzzled
What was it that was missing from the mastery of this art?
What was missing to bring life back into this soil?
What happened that the clay never survived?

Maybe the loving songs she whispered
        Maybe it was the unique scent of her hands!

And when you put your hands on my face

I become weightless
I fly...

I feel your absence.
Ah! How I miss the smell of your hands...

The second butterfly flied away confidently to approach this unknown beauty. There was no way he could tolerate this endless magnitude of sorrow in his flower's glorious face. He was too involved with her to sit and just watch. He got close and closer. To know everything about the candle, you should see it from up close. He got as close as he could but as soon as he felt the warmth on the corner of his colorful wing, he was frightened and flew back towards his beloved flower.

He Felt so brave and content to have more to tell her than the first butterfly. Happy with his success, he began the story of how it was to meet the light in such a close distance.

There were tears in her eye!

There should be more!

What can possibly feed the hunger of the flower for the love of the candle?

The little that he brought for her from the candle didn't light up her world and the cascade of tears started to fall from her shining eyes.

She wasn't satisfied and she murmured to herself, you haven't learned anything about candle light.

There are times in life that it seems we have lost our connection with the entire universe but on a higher level we are building new connections.

That is when the evolution starts, when you hear the loud scream of your soul- you peel, you purify.

That is when the most extraordinary thoughts and philosophies of life come into existence.

What comes out of those bitter moments
                        is the sweetest fruit
            and what is life all about?
        Coming to taste the bitter sweetness of that fruit one day?
                        What complicated beings we are!

And night veiled the dark blue of the sky in black!

I was gazing at the image of the glorious moon in the limited frame of a quiet separated lagoon, happy that I could touch the moon.

     And you crossed my way
         like sand
             that drops in the water,
                 and you took the stillness of my
lagoon away.

Raise your head!
     Look directly at the sky!
         Watch the moon not through your earthy small frame of the lagoon which can lose its clarity by a single grain of sand.

Find the moon in the vast field of the sky! Dare to look at the beauty directly in the face!

And how many times did I try to take my eyes away from the beauty of your face!

Come to me!

Come before the goddess of dream wakes me up.

Together, let's bring the spring!

Let us not wait until the winter snows upon our land.

We can guard the blossoms together.
         We can guard our forbidden love
           And our dreams!

There were other hands,
                more capable than ours…

There were other hands, those that put me on your way to look
into your amorous eyes.

And how a glance from your charming eyes
                enslaved me,
                        enticed my soul,
                                enamored my heart,
                and left me forever unconscious and drunk.

I can smell your scent on the wind.
                Everything echoes your velvet voice.
                        What color is your sky?
                Are you dreaming or are you awake, my love?

The last butterfly that was watching this scene was the smallest of all.

This flower was her entire world.

When she first cracked her cocoon and opened her eyes to this world, she fell on the velvet leaves of this flower.

She was the first thing that her skin had touched,
 the first beauty that her eyes had seen,
the first smell that went through her soul,
the first creature that she felt love for.

The flower was her first impression of this entire life and it was the love of this flower that had been so tightly woven into the fabric of her delicate wings. It gave her enough strength to experience the amazement of opening up her wings and flying.

Of course her heart was too small to afford the extreme torment of seeing her flower's tearful eyes.

She was all ears to what the other butterflies were telling her and she was admiring them for their extended effort and their exceptional courage in traveling towards the light and to almost touching it and for bringing stories about it. However, her heart was broken when she saw the sorrowful face of her beloved flower who was longing to hear more and more of her beloved candle.

You are drown in the sea
And I am drown in you
This sea was the metaphor of your being.
I was the surfer,
          you were the sea.
                    You vividly breath.
                              It's your nature to be wild
               you never cease challenging me
                    with your giant waves,
                         but every time I got lost
                    in the endless tunnels of your being,
                         I could feel the gentle touch of your hands
guiding me to the end,
          even through those deep wrinkles on your wild beautiful
face, I could see
          your worried eyes staring at me.
                    I heard you
               every time you whispered to yourself :
               I don't want to drown you in me, I want you alive.

What a pain to be a butterfly and to be in love with a flower! What an unreachable love.

But still, she was fortunate, she had wings, she could fly. Nothing was impossible in her world. She was able to see the flower, the love of her life.

She could see her beloved flower any time and from any where on earth, nothing could stop her to nest her agitated soul in the sweet calm of her arms...

How hard it is to be a flower,
          rooted in the soil
               and to be in love with an unreachable light
                       in another part of the soil!

This was the least she could do, to see the light from deep inside, from the closest possible!

One should feel the light.
          should become one with the light,
               One should become the light
                    to be able to say
                       what it is like to be a candle light.

Becoming one with oneself
Before the quest
for becoming one
With the beloved one!

Far from you,

Still

Falling for you...

Seeing the trembling rays of the light from a distance
she flapped her wings stronger and stronger,

So this was the light,

The light that the flower has talked about and truly, what a shining
beauty is this light that has captured my flower's heart.

She flaps her wings, hypnotized by the rising flame of the burning
candle.
She was gazing at the rainbow of colors inside the flame.
The shape of the flame was like a tear drop.

She flew towards it and she got closer and closer she was too taken
by this enormous beauty.

She was changed by the experience and not conscious enough to
realize that she was getting too close.

And the closer she got the more she felt the gentle warmth of the
candle on her arms.

She was gliding above and around the flame, watching it, and
wondering why the candle was crying too…

Rivers of tears were falling from her eyes.

Was she in love? Was it a forbidden love?
To keep the flame and light, maybe that is the whole purpose of
their existence,
to light the small circle of their surrounding.

What if the candle knows
that the blaze of her light
has traveled miles and miles away
to a distant deserted land
into the untouched depth
of a flower's heart
who, by itself, is a true shinning
    diamond
sitting in the heart of the ring of
    three butterflies...

When did I fall away from you?
When did I fall so in love with you?
Who knows,
maybe we are the missing heroes
of someone else's book.
Where is that border between dream and reality?

Either we are walking asleep in this real world
Or we are sleeping but awake in another world.
Which one is dream?
Which one is reality?
Maybe we are just a dream
Appearing in another dream?

Wake up my love!
Or wake me up!

And the little butterfly of the story cried louder and louder.

Her heart was touched by the meaningful love of the flower for the candle and the existence of this light.

She approached the candle to hold her shimmering light in her own arms and to touch with her entire being this flame.

But the fire was too rebellious to be held in her arms...

The flame got through to her delicate body
and in a second, enflamed her colorful being into nothing...

and all that was heard in the whole universe
 was only a quiet crackle of fire
              and forever, she disappeared.

There was no turning back to tell the beloved flower any of what she had observed and any of how she felt.

The only one who ventured to touch the flame never came back.

She became one with the flame.

The one who got to know everything never came back...

Even the story teller
        Fell asleep.
                She is still awake
                        With her open eyes
                                still searching for a way
                                        beyond the clouds!

It is said that there once was a nightingale who sat on the edge of a lagoon to ease her tremendous thirst by drinking from that clear water. When she dipped her little beak into the water, she faced a breathtakingly beautiful bird in the water, a charming combination of delicacy and colors, with a meticulously sculpted body and wings. She couldn't take her eyes away from her; she was mute and shocked. She stepped back from the lagoon and flew away.

It is said that this little bird never drank from that water and never wet her dry beak and she fell in love with that unknown beauty in the water.

She escaped all her life from that image and ever since then she sits on the tallest trees and tirelessly sings the voice of her heart.

What if she knew
        that she was in love
                with the simple reflection of her own beauty?

That bird flew and sang around the flower all night .
My beloved flower!
Stay awake!
Lest the careless dream
	take the awareness from your eyes!
Lest you sleep
  and the butterflies take that sweet extract away from your soul.
Lest the sleep
	bends the stature of your beauty!
Lest you sleep
	and the yellow leaves of the tired trees
		fall on your shoulders!
Lest a careless hand
	plucks you away from yourself!
Lest the pale yellow color of this autumn
		reflects in your red rose face.
Lest this cold autumn breeze
		trembles your body and your delicate soul!
Stay awake my love!
	My ever green flower!

It is said that from the loving songs of that bird all the sleeping flowers of the orchard woke up one after another asking each other what is the nightingale singing for?

Maybe this is just a dream and we are hearing songs in our dream!

Isn't it that all the singing birds
		left town?
And once again, the garden woke up in the middle of autumn sleep.

All the flowers
	Except that one shining flower
		That didn't believe in blooming in fall !

No one knows
on that cold autumn night
     what was said
       and what was heard,
Between the singing bird
        and the beloved blooming flower.

When night gave birth to the light of day

The passer by found a flower drown in dew drops
     and the lifeless delicate body of a broken winged bird
      drown in blood.

Did she cross the sea?

Every one was amazed by the swift line of flight.
                    And I am drawn
                            In the red trace
                                    That was left behind!
                                            She crossed the sea!

And this
        became another fairy tale
                to fill the empty nights of the children of our world.

I wonder,
How on the brown wrinkled body of trees
Grow the most colorful blooms?

Like life
that blossoms
in the wrinkled face
of a new born baby.

What if I lost you!
Would it be possible to still stay in love
without having you to love?

I am flowing
In the falling rivers of thoughts.
Still falling for you …
I see myself
Fading away…
Come back to me !
Come beside me! Before I sleep …

I fell asleep…
     I saw a dream,
I dreamt
     that I was riding on a shooting star
Paving my way
     outside the sky.

I picked up our moon

I freed her from the sky.

I stole the sun
     from the plain surface of the sky.
I carried the lights of the world
     in the small palm of my hands
And I left a dust trail of light behind
     In the empty sky of our land
     and I disappeared.
I traveled and traveled for many light years,
     but
Outside our milky way,
     Away from our sky
     No one knew
     What the moon was.
     There were
     thousands and thousands of suns
     among the stars…

Believing you is impossible

Even in dreams...

I have never been to this place!

Larks are playfully chasing the hawks.

I am floating in a mysterious silence.

The ground is full of falling stars.

There is the moon, there is the sun; the sky is clear of clouds and I have a view of all the stars.

I am floating, I am weightless, I have a pulse.

Yellow and green are sitting together.

The whole orchard is blossoming with life

I feel the breeze,
    I recognize this aroma in the air!

 I am not tired
        I am awake.
                The road is paved with red rose petals…

        Is it spring?
Is it fall?

I am standing on top of a solid mountain
higher than where the stars fall,
           higher than where they shine.

I see the sun , but I see the stars…
           Is it finally day?
                Is it still night?

Sky, earth, sun, moon, birds, trees, rivers, seas- they all share the same bed. Is there anyone in here to tell me if I am dreaming or if I am alive?

I can't see. My eyes are full of tears, and I still have a candle in my hand...

Am I alive?

What if you show me the sparkle of the star in the sky
    And leave me on this earth with a fading glow of a fire fly?
What if you let me taste the water of your fountain
        And leave me alone
          beside a swamp on a far away plain?
What if you tame my wild soul
        And leave me defenseless
           In the middle of this wild world?
What if you stepped out
       And you broke all the glass walls behind
         By closing hard the door of my heart?
What if my madness for you
       that captured the magnificence of my whole life
         Becomes only a form of madness
           to your eyes…

What do I do then?

Here is a shining mirror to behold
your forgotten image.

You were the only image that I ever
had reflected in my life.

Welcome my love
    To the fifth season of your life.
        After winter and fall
            It is the season of pure love.

I existed for years through your eyes.
    This is where green perpetuates forever.
        Maybe it is time to reflect your own image!

I see myself flying over the fields of wild flowers…Someone is strumming the strings of my heart. I know this song!

There is an end to this autumn,
Changing seasons
And spring starts...

Did I ever exist?

I hear the loud sound of someone's steps …
Someone is walking on the glass floor of my heart…
I feel my heart tremble, it shivers, it aches.
It's me walking on my heart.
I smoothly walk through my heart . Lest I break my heart !
You are there.
I can still feel you in there!

I have embraced you in my heart.
        For years I hid you in my heart.
        I walk towards you,
                I take you in my arms
            And I cry for one last time.
I see myself
    with love
        Walking you
            Out of my heart…

Ah!
It was the shadow of our own Earth
                    Covering
                        The shining body of the moon
                                in the sky...

It was the cast of her own dark shadow
        Drawing a crescent of a smile
                On the far face of the moon in the sky.

What is my heart made of
      that it trembles with your look,
           Melts with your touch,
            beats for your love,
               and breaks by your sulking?

And I gave up everything
              While stepping her out of my heart
                    Everything
                    Even
                        the beats of my heart...

Ah! I can't believe
            I got free.
                I breath.
                    I exist.
                        I am alive.

The beauty of **Freedom** has once again captured my soul.

The universe has become my stage!

And I,
        still marveling at life's greatest wonders and joys.

The life force is once again filling my soul
            with a world of fresh air

                    and I,
                        happier than always
                            am more than before alive!

I hope
    by turning this last page
        the soft breeze
            which touched my face
                comes out
                    and kisses your eyes.

I hope
    one day
        You will clear all the clouds
            From your world
            With the magnificent blue of your eyes!

                    I will miss you my love…

LaVergne, TN USA
24 March 2011
221517LV00009B/43/A